Grumpy Granny Grumble

Written by
Jean Richardson

Illustrated by
Nancy Peterson

Grumpy Granny's
Book of Good Manners

FIRST EDITION
Copyright © 1999
By Jean Richardson

McKinley View Publishing
P.O. Box 13314
Trapper Creek, Alaska 99683
(907) 733-1555
www.mckinleyviewlodge.com

Fourth printing

ISBN 978-1-57168-306-9 (hard bound)
ISBN 978-1-57168-135-5 (perfect bound)

Printed by Everbest Printing Investment Ltd., Guangzhou, China,
through **Alaska Print Brokers**, Anchorage, Alaska.

Library of Congress Cataloging-in-Publication Data

Richardson, Jean.
   Grumpy Granny Grumble's book of manners / written by Jean Richardson; illustrated by Nancy Peterson. — 1st. ed.
      p.   cm.
   Summary: Humorous illustrations and rhyming text provide guidance on the proper way to behave in all sorts of situations.
      ISBN: 978-1-57168-306-9 (hard bound) & 978-1-57168-135-5 (perfect bound)
   1. Etiquette for children and youth. [1. Etiquette. 2. Behavior.] I. Peterson, Nancy Garnet, ill. II. Title
BJ1857.C5R43 1999
395.1'22--dc21

                                                                                     99-17525
                                                                                        CIP

This book is dedicated to my Grandson Taylor,
who never ever makes his Granny Grumpy!

To Miriam and Lydia ~

With love from Gran

and Pappy! ☺

Jean Carey Richardson

A lady lives in our town
Who is gentle, sweet, and kind,
But children with bad manners
Can make Granny lose her mind.

Granny's from the old school
Where good manners rule supreme.
When children use good manners
You will see Granny beam.

But when they use bad manners,
If they're rude and impolite,
Then sweet old Granny Grumble
Gets so mad that she could fight.

So here's a little list of rules
For you to keep in mind.
Just follow these directions,
You'll be proper, neat, and kind.

Never laugh at others who look different
For you see,
Underneath the surface
They're the same as you and me.

If you think it's clever
When shopping at the mall
To scratch yourself upon the rump,
You might make Granny bawl.

When chewing gum be careful
That it's safely thrown away.
Don't leave it on the sidewalk
To ruin someone else's day.

There is nothing so disgusting,
Any Granny knows,
As to see a small child trying
To pick "Boogers" from his nose.

And as for sounds annoying,
Oh my goodness! Gracious me!
Those make Granny Grumble
Just start crying in her tea.

While waiting in a long line
It really isn't nice
To cut in front of others.
You may have to pay a price.

Granny says it doesn't matter
If you win or lose the game,
But if you show poor sportsmanship
You'll put your team to shame.

When eating at the table
Granny Grumble says beware
Not to burp so loudly
That it curls your neighbor's hair.

And of course you all remember
To chew your food with care—
Keep your food upon your own plate,
No one else will want to share.

Straws are marvelous inventions.
They really are quite nice.
Just don't make those slurping noises
When you're down to air and ice.

"Excuse me" is the magic phrase
That let's you pass with ease
Through groups of folks that otherwise
Might give your neck a squeeze.

Be careful where you're stepping,
Especially in line,
For the foot on which you're stomping
Might possibly be mine!

When in parks or public places
Having fun's the thing to do,
But be careful not to bother
Other folks who share the view.

When you are through playing
Please put your toys away.
They could cause lots of trouble
Left in other people's way.

Don't comb your hair in public,
In cafes or movie shows,
For the people seated 'round you
Don't want your hair up their nose.

Granny loves polite words
Such as "Thank you, Ma'am,"
and "Please."
You will see Granny grinning
When you use words like these.

Grumpy Granny Grumble
Is as pleased as she can be
When someone holds the door for her
And treats her courteously.

Respond when someone says "Hello."
It's really not polite
To turn your head the other way
Until they're out of sight.

Remember truth is golden
No matter what you do.
A lie can turn against you
And shame you through and through.

If you think it's funny
To cheat your friends at play,
Be sure to watch behind you—
Justice usually has its way.

So if you have a Granny
She'll be happy, you will find,
If you keep these rules of living
Always foremost in your mind.

If every single person
Was as nice as he could be
To every other person,
What a great world this would be!